SECRETS OF the KINGDOM

SECRETS OF THE KINGDOM

FR. RICHARD HO LUNG, M.O.P.

MISSIONARIES OF THE POOR
KINGSTON

SAINT BENEDICT PRESS
Charlotte, North Carolina

Quotations from Scripture are from the Revised Standard Version (Catholic Edition).

Book design by A.R.T. Services, Christopher J. Pelicano and Abby M. Pelicano.

Cataloguing-in-publication data on file with the Library of Congress.

ISBN: 978-1-61890-401-0

Published in the United States by
Saint Benedict Press, LLC
P.O. Box 410487
Charlotte, NC 28241
www.tanbooks.com

Printed and bound in the United States of America.

I dedicate this book to Christ Crucified,
my one and only friend,
beloved brother and savior God.

Contents

INTRODUCTION

In a world that engages and demands our full attention, it is difficult to pray and attend to the depths of the inner soul. Yet there you will find unlimited riches and indeed Christ himself, the hidden treasure, so precious and so beautiful, though forgotten and even discarded by modern people.

The richness of life can only be estimated by those who know intimately and deeply the truth of the presence of Christ, whom we carry within us like a mother with her child. This truth is inextricably bound up with our very being. This, the most valuable aspect of our lives, is the greatest gift given to each of us human persons. It is the *pearl of great price*, and I would like us all to seek no other riches.

We nurture this gift in us, the *pearl of great price*, the *treasure in the field*, and determine never to loose it; not even death, nor the threat of death, will separate us from the Lord. We pray and reflect on his presence enriched by the Word of God, which carries within it the Eucharist, in which he dwells and the experiences we have as we seek to build his Kingdom.

Meditation is the descent into the womb—our innermost self - where Christ dwells: ***"you are the temple of the Holy Spirit."*** Each of us has Christ in the depth of our being. But we need to reflect silently, daily, or even more often, and be at one with Him in the wedding chamber of our soul.

Once we know of his presence and we turn to him in all our life experiences inside and outside of ourselves, we find him over and over again. He is the truth of life, and he shows us the way to the fullness of the spiritual life. He reveals the *Secrets of the Kingdom* as we live and labour and become true sons and daughters of God—in days full of darkness or light.

Contemplation leads us to action, and the more we act for and within the kingdom, the more we discover that every word and action of our Lord's is absolute truth, intense and irrevocable truth that is important to us.

As we live out the life of Christ, it develops and increases our faith. Rather than being infant

Christians, we become mature Christians, ready to be one with him on the cross which, as a result, leads to eternal life.

There is a woman, Grace Washington, who has been our volunteer and associate for nearly 30 years. She is one of my closest friends and she has gleaned these meditations from the talks I have given. It is a compilation I would never have done and I am humbled that Grace considered it worthy and useful for others who wish to satisfy their search for the secrets of the Kingdom. Then there is Sue-Ann Howell to whom I am also indebted for having chosen the scripture verses that correlate with these selections. I am also grateful for Don Drumm (dondrummstudios.com) who provided the beautiful interior images.

In this book I endeavour to share my insights and experiences with you. I hope that they will resonate within you and lead you to prayer. Take your time with each vignette. Spend time on your inner being.

Faith is dark and sometimes blinding, but God is always there. You will find him, and you will find yourself in a new way, and you will be deeply satisfied that you have responded to the Lord's call: ***"Come, follow me."***

1

One With God

YOU MUST ESTABLISH a dynamic relationship
with the Lord
whereby all day long you and the Lord are talking
with each other.
when you really believe in the Lord
when you really trust the Lord and his intimacy
with you
when you really know that the Lord is there,
he is never out of sight, he is never separated
from you
you carry him with you everywhere you go.
there is no such thing as loneliness with God.

FOR I AM SURE that neither death, nor life, nor angels, nor principalities, nor things present, nor things to come, nor powers, nor height, nor depth, nor anything else in all creation, will be able to separate us from the love of God in Christ Jesus our Lord.

— *ROMANS 8:38-39*

2

All For Him

PRAY AND WORK in the Lord
pray from the depths
pray from the depths of your inner self
where the Holy Spirit dwells
from the depths love the Lord, work for the Lord
live for the Lord from the depths.

let the Holy Spirit work through you
with you and in you
you will find him lifting you up
your labour will be light (his yoke is sweet)
as you labour to build his Kingdom.

his work as your food will make you strong
as you build his Kingdom
his hand upon your hand
his heart within your heart
your mind will be enlightened by his wisdom
his eternal peace.

THEREFORE, MY BELOVED brethren, be steadfast, immovable, always abounding in the work of the Lord, knowing that in the Lord your labor is not in vain.

— 1 CORINTHIANS 15:58

3

Enter In

WELCOME INTO THE LOVE of the Lord,
enter into his heart
he shall be your soul
you shall abide in him forever
every heartbeat of his shall be yours
his every desire shall be yours
life will flow between you and him
he will be your home
and he will be your love
he will reveal himself through you
you shall enjoy the deepest happiness
and peace in the house of the Lord

BY THIS WE KNOW that we abide in him and he in us, because he has given us of his own Spirit.

— 1 JOHN 4:13

4

The Divine Indwelling

THE LIVING GOD calls us
in the ground of our being
in the stillness
we must recall ourselves
from everything and everywhere
the one who prays is gathered
in quietness and inner alertness
the true self,
the center of power, substantial and everlasting,
God unites himself with us there
the inner self,
the tabernacle of every human person,
the place within where God dwells,
it is the holy of holies

BUT WHEN YOU PRAY, go into your room and shut the door and pray to your Father who is in secret; and your Father who sees in secret will reward you.

— *MATTHEW 6:6*

5

Listen To Him

TRUTH SPEAKS WITHIN US without the outward sound of words

incline my heart to the words of your mouth,
oh Lord,
I want to hear you, you by yourself, carefully
instruct me
you teach and enlighten the very heart.
it is you who makes me bear fruit
you unfold what you want
you kindle the flame within.

do not let me be ranked among those who
heard the Word but did not obey it,
believed it but failed to keep it

AND I WILL PRAY the Father, and he will give you another Counselor, to be with you forever, the Spirit of truth, whom the world cannot receive, because it neither sees him nor knows him; you know him, for he dwells with you, and will be in you.

—JOHN 14:16-17

6

Endless Love

PRAYER IS THE ACT of love with God
we are united with God in the depths of ourselves
not in the mind
because the mind grasps
only with reason and logic
only the heart experiences God.

if we pray from the depths,
we receive more and more
the presence of the Lord

there is no limit
that the Lord has placed upon
what he will give us
and the wonder is that
the more we give ourselves to the Lord
the more we are able to give ourselves to others

BUT AS IT IS written, "What no eye has seen, nor ear heard, nor the heart of man conceived, what God has prepared for those who love him,"

— 1 CORINTHIANS 2:9

7

Seek God's Will

DEAR LORD, YOU ARE the Creator of
the world
and you know all things
you made all things according to your purpose
your will for all creation is revealed
in the nature, in the heart, in the soul of things
all things have a purpose, which is to glorify you
by revealing and fulfilling their inner purpose
you created the world, and you created our minds
and wills.
our minds are made to seek your will;
our wills are made to be placed under your will
so we will work according to your plan,
and according to your will,
for all of us and for all things. You are the
Creator, Lord,
you know your purpose and reason for all things.
as your creatures, we are called in freedom to
choose
your will over our own will, and to choose

your will over any person's will
those who seek your will and only your will
are truly people of God.

DO NOT BE CONFORMED to this world but be transformed by the renewal of your mind, that you may prove what is the will of God, what is good and acceptable and perfect.

— *ROMANS 12:2*

8

Focus On Him

I AM BETWEEN the world and my Lord
I am a divided self
between the world and the Kingdom of God.
I am divided; rescue me, oh Lord,
stretched out on the Cross,
let your hands reach out and save me!

constantly my mind and my flesh
wander away to the cares of the world in which
    we live
bring me back, call me back,
lest I perish in the kingdom of the flesh, in the
    kingdom of Satan.

let me live in you,
safe from the passions of the world
that keep calling me, that keep tempting me
to forego your love
that nails me to the Cross of Christ,
            to the poor and the Church,
            to hatred and rejection,

and hearing nothing but your voice,
and your promises,
which I sometimes hear
but do not hear so clearly

FOR THE SON of man came to
seek and to save the lost.

— *LUKE 19:10*

9

Forsake Him Not

I CANNOT DEPART from you, Lord.
how many times have I sinned?
but you pursued me with love
I thought you would desert me.
Surprisingly! You are still here,
stirring deep within me, holding me,
loving me, directing me with your love.

I ask, "Why haven't you deserted me?
I am so undeserving.
get away from me, Lord; leave me!
you should forsake me, as I have forsaken you,"

yet, Lord, here you are beside me,
within and all around,
my heart and my mind
surrounded with your love.

yearning for the one true God,
Lord, I cannot depart from you.

BUT THE LORD is faithful; he will strengthen you and guard you from evil.

— 2 THESSALONIANS 3:3

10

Fill Us With Love

LORD, WE CALL upon your name,
without you we are empty
you come to us so readily,
so readily—we can't believe it
you care for us sinners, so weak
we are nothing, yet you surround us
suddenly there is warmth within,
and as we dwell with you
and pray with sleepy eyes,
you are present within.
no longer like a dead dry leaf
that has fallen and been taken away by the wind
for your breath makes our hearts beat
and warms us with love and peace
even while we sleep under your wings
in the arms of our Savior, we gain the strength
of our Lord, our God and our King
our spirits cry out aloud in a dream
and with the angels we sing

BUT IF ONE loves God, one is known by him.

— 1 CORINTHIANS 8:3

11

Believe In Him

BEING IMPERFECT IN our capability
is not a deterrent in prayer
we need filial boldness.

"Whatever you ask for in prayer,
believe that you receive it, and you
will."

such is the power of prayer and of faith
that one does not doubt

"All things are possible with God"

you must leave your life at the disposal of God
to get done that for which you pray

REJOICE IN YOUR hope, be patient in tribulation, be constant in prayer.

— *ROMANS 12:12*

12

Know Thyself

SELF-KNOWLEDGE REQUIRES that we
identify who we are
what we have been
what we are called to be

we need to look at our past and
the patterns it has imprinted on our souls
we need to know the acts that
have been most deeply entrenched in us

our love of the world
our love of money
our love of security
our desire to achieve
our desire to satisfy even our loved ones

what we have now is the present and the future
what will we be today?
what will we do today?
tomorrow, what do we wish to achieve

for ourselves, for our loved ones, for the world?
do we truly wish to build a world
that is full of light and goodness?

I CAN DO all things in him who strengthens me.

— *PHILIPPIANS 4:13*

13

A Christ-Centered Life

YOUR MEDITATION IS your soul's content
your purpose is your vision
your desire is your treasure
your goal is your dream

make sure it is not the world
make sure it is not the self
but the inner man, Christ himself,
who is the soul's content

the vision, the purpose
the ideal of the real self
must be Christ himself, the Lord
destined to be crucified and to live forever

FOR YOU HAVE died, and your
life is hid with Christ in God.

— *COLOSSIANS 3:3*

14

More Is Less

THE MORE YOU LOVE the world
the less you love God

the more you love God
the more you reject the world

the more you love yourself
the less you love others

the more centered you are on yourself
the less you are centered on God

the more you possess this world
the less you possess of eternal life

which do you choose?

AND YOU SHALL love the Lord your God with all your heart, and with all your soul, and with all your mind, and with all your strength.

— *MARK 12:30*

15

Father Knows Best

I OVERHEARD THE QUESTIONS asked, why
shouldn't I have
the best, why shouldn't my family have the best?

in fact, you should have the best, but not
the best of
the material world, rather the best that there
is in life,
which will be given you by the Lord,

the greatest happiness
peace of mind
understanding and wisdom
the genuine and true meaning of
love

IF YOU THEN, who are evil, know how to give good gifts to your children, how much more will your Father who is in heaven give good things to those who ask him!

— *MATTHEW 7:11*

16

Spirit Matters

WE MUST PRAY that we have eyes to see,
ears to hear,
and hearts that not only beat, but pound with love
in a time when we seek to live longer than God
intends,
the importance of spirit
—the heart that loves—
is of infinite value, more so than a long life
a long life can be dull and spiritless
though the limbs walk and the lungs breathe.
Science cannot create the spirit of life,
which is the spirit of self-sacrifice and service

THIS IS MY commandment,
that you love one another as I have
loved you.

— *JOHN 15:12*

17

Step Out In Faith

FAITH IS VERY DARK and frightening
most uncomfortable, it is a
passageway in which we see little light
but a prompting inside of us says
go forward, go forward
we hear a voice, and we're in a strange
land and dark terrain and, like
Magdalene, we follow the whisper of the heart

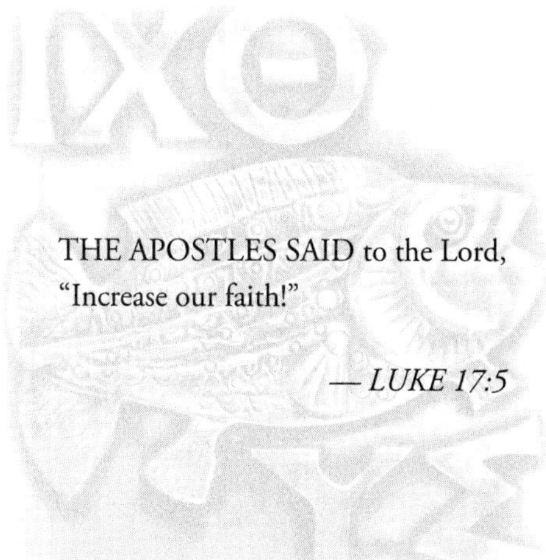

THE APOSTLES SAID to the Lord,
"Increase our faith!"

— *LUKE 17:5*

18

God's Love Is Eternal

THIS PASSING WORLD, so beautiful:

the flowers, the birds of the air;
the music, the laughter,
the sunlight, and starlight.

they dazzle; they stir within, the inner soul of things.
but all things pass, only Christ our Lord remains
while the flowers fade and the birds no longer sing.

when the music cries and laughter dies,
and night descends,
the inner flame burns
in the tired heart and mind
worn by years of watching and waiting,
loving and longing,
something emerges, concentrated and hard—

The Rock.

EVERYONE THEN WHO HEARS these words of mine and does them will be like a wise man who built his house upon the rock.

— *MATTHEW 7:24*

19

Multiply Your Love

I WANT YOU TO love the Lord
I want you to love the sweetness of his love for
you.
                    you love the Lord but not enough.
there is so much more love in you than you think,
there is so much more in him for you to love
give your love to the most adorable wounds of
Christ's wounded humanity, which daily suffers
  and dies
                    love is a miracle force,
                    you need not portion out your love
                    it will multiply
the more we love the more we are able to love
until the world overflows with the risen Christ

BUT GROW IN THE GRACE and knowledge of our Lord and Savior Jesus Christ.

— 2 PETER 3:18

20

Give All To God

I KNOW YOUR WORKS: you are neither hot nor cold.
Would that you were either cold or hot!

Revelation warns us to beware of being mediocre
do not be a mediocre Christian, a compromising
Christian or a rationalizing Christian
you either seek first the Lord or you don't
if you are satisfied, it is because you don't love
the Lord

when you love the Lord and the Lord loves you
he will never stop until he has consumed you with
his love, he'll take away everything from you
and then give you everything that he is
but it requires your losing your life

FOR WHOEVER WOULD save his life will lose it; and whoever loses his life for my sake and the gospel's will save it.

— *MARK 8:35*

21

Aiming For Battle

TRUTH IS THE physician's knife
truth is the light
shining on our sins, to give light
so we can see
so we can heal,
so we can be humble and whole,
pure and simple before God
so we can be children again
so we can be aware of the struggle and battle
of our sinful selves, yearning and wanting
the true self and the Lord
above all,
and become warriors
battling to defeat our evil selves
and win souls
as we have won the battle within our souls

STAND THEREFORE, HAVING GIRDED your loins with truth, and having put on the breastplate of righteousness, and having shod your feet with the equipment of the gospel of peace; besides all these, taking the shield of faith, with which you can quench all the flaming darts of the evil one. And take the helmet of salvation, and the sword of the Spirit, which is the word of God.

— *EPHESIANS 6:14-17*

22

Labor For Light

STRUGGLE TOGETHER for truth
find the truth and live it
live it till it hurts
live it till others cry out, no more
live it till you are martyred by your own
    loved ones
and you will bring forth
saints and holy men and women
God's new Kingdom
new wine in new skins
drawn from the old
respectful of tradition
a light that burns brightly
Christ the light of lights,
the light that burns forever and ever

FIGHT THE GOOD FIGHT of the faith; take hold of the eternal life to which you were called when you made the good confession in the presence of many witnesses.

— 1 TIMOTHY 6:12

23

Never Give Up

WE MUST NEVER be inattentive
we must not stop trying,
that is what love is all about
that is God's love
that we keep on trying
learning to love
learning by trying to love
though it is difficult and painful
that is God's love

and thus we keep trying to the end
loving one, then many, then all
while telling the truth
hurting others and being hurt by others
at the foot of the Cross
dying to ourselves, crucifying others
but staying by his feet
wounding, but loving
purifying one another
and being purified

by God's love
and God's deep faith in us
and God carrying us to the end

FOR WHATEVER IS BORN of God overcomes the world; and this is the victory that overcomes the world, our faith.

— 1 JOHN 5:4

24

Live Out The Beatitudes

LIVE OUT YOUR FAITH, not simply go to
Mass,
not simply go to the adoration chapel, not simply
say the rosary and not simply battle causes,
but above all live out the beatitudes,
open up your hearts, be a force of people who
wash each other's feet, that is the living Gospel

fill the valleys with that new song
fill the valleys with that messenger that John the
Baptist is.
let the world see that there is a Christianity
that is active and alive and changing the world

HERE IS A CALL for the endurance of the saints, those who keep the commandments of God and the faith of Jesus.

— *REVELATION 14:12*

25

Called To Be Like Christ

POPE JOHN PAUL SAID the Church of the
poor is the true
Church and the Church of the poor is the Church
at its best
you need not flee from your beautiful churches
but you
must understand that you cannot escape the call
of Christ:

"I have come to bring good news to
the poor."

in the Scriptures there is Christ, page to page,
chapter
to chapter, almost verse to verse, concerned
with the
blind and the lepers and the widows and the
orphans
and the forgotten ones and the sinners

how can you as Christians not recognize that you must be caught up in that same work, you are called
to be oriented toward service of the broken and wounded body of Jesus in the world today

AND JESUS LOOKING UPON him loved him, and said to him, "You lack one thing; go, sell what you have, and give to the poor, and you will have treasure in heaven; and come, follow me."

— *MARK 10:21*

26

The Life Of Christ

EMBRACE FULLY the life of Jesus Christ
you cannot be satisfied until you
have been transformed into the life of Christ
Jesus gives you his Body and his Blood
you have the blood of Jesus in your veins
you carry the flesh of Jesus in your body
you have everything given to you by the Lord
he calls you by grace everyday to be
united with him in that sacrifice and to
bring the light of Christ to all

Christianity is not an idle thing
it is the way of life in the fullest

IN HIM WAS life, and the life was the light of men.

—*JOHN 1:4*

27

A Living Faith

THE CHRISTIAN FAITH becomes hypocritical
form without content, appearance without reality
without the beatitudes and works with the poor
and sinners
Christ pointed us all to the Cross

"Bear each other's burdens"
"Take up the cross daily"
"Sell all you have and give to the poor"
"Wash each other's feet"

no longer is religion just outward appearances
and form
but it is given a goal, a vision of life,
a content, substantial truth, and a way to live
religion and reality become united
in the Kingdom of God here on earth

I DO IT ALL for the sake of the gospel, that I may share in its blessings.

— 1 CORINTHIANS 9:23

28

Christ Truly Present

IF ONLY WE COULD understand
Christianity is not meant to be notional
but to be faith in action
the heart of Jesus is always large enough
to bind every bitter wound
and to heal every broken spirit

"Blessed are the poor"
"Blessed are those who mourn."

in the very heart of tears,
in the very heart of sickness, poverty, death,
we find the presence of the Lord
and the blessings of the Lord

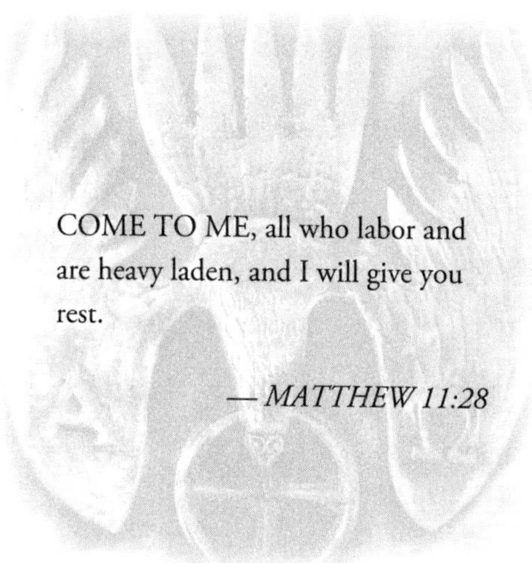

COME TO ME, all who labor and are heavy laden, and I will give you rest.

— *MATTHEW 11:28*

29

Teach Me, Lord

OH, LORD, TEACH ME the truth,
teach me the truth of life,
teach me the truth of Christ,
teach me who he is,
and what I am meant to be

teach me the truth of his words,
the application of his words,
how they apply to my reality,
and to my everyday life

may his Spirit surround me,
mould me, make me,
and infuse me with his truth,
with his love, with the true meaning of life
and what I am to be

AND YOU WILL know the truth,
and the truth will make you free.

— *JOHN 8:32*

30

One With Christ

LOOK ON Christ
gaze on him
see him
understand him
hear his every word
and let him work in your heart

stand before the crucifix
pray and commit yourself to Christ
remembering that as
you commit yourself to Christ
you commit yourself to a way of life
that the world does not understand,
that you sacrifice yourself for others

AND HE SAID to all, "If any man would come after me, let him deny himself and take up his cross daily and follow me."

— *LUKE 9:23*

31

Truth Brings Light

MIRACLES ARE DONE day by day
if only we would believe
if only we would have faith in that Cross of Christ
if only we would allow the truth to emerge
from the depth of ourselves
even though the truth is a very heavy cross
even though the love that has to be offered to our
  broken world
is a very heavy cross
even though truth and love,
that husband and wife of spiritual values,
have to be borne right up to Calvary
and then the joy,
and then the light breaks forth from us

ALL THINGS ARE POSSIBLE to
him who believes.

— *MARK 9:23*

32

Our Savior Within

CHRIST LIVES in us
we need to understand this and seek him
past all our foolishness
past all superficial values
then we will come to Bethlehem
and we will kneel before the Lord, and
we will find in this mysterious, humble child,
in the flesh of this little one,
the divine light.

Would it not be a wonderful thing
if in our lifetimes, we discovered in
the agony and the confusion of life
this divine light
this beautiful thing that is centered
in our very hearts.

O THE DEPTHS OF the riches
and wisdom and knowledge of God!
How unsearchable are his judgments
and how inscrutable his ways!

— *ROMANS 11:33*

33

Give All To God

WHAT DO YOU WANT to do by the end of
your life?

Is it not to have poured out everything that
you are?
To have given all that has been given to you back
to the Lord?
To have used up everything that the Lord has
dispensed to you?
To have squeezed all that there is in life as an
offering to the Lord?
To have loved until you couldn't possibly love
anymore?
To have loved to the last drop of your blood?
Of your mind? Of your intelligence? Of your
strength?
To the last day of your life?

Isn't that the point? Why restrain and hold back?

YOU SHALL LOVE the Lord your God with all your heart, and with all your soul, and with all your strength, and with all your mind; and your neighbor as yourself.

— LUKE 10:27

34

Two Become One

TEACH US TO BE serious, Lord,
so serious that we gaze upon your face
and become transformed by love,
your love for us, and our love for you
so we'll bear your wounds,
your sadness and distress,
labor unto death, and find you in our poor.

Teach us the meaning of life
in your words, in your wounds
so that our hearts are your heart,
our minds are your mind,
and nothing exists in us, but you alone, oh Lord
we will eat of your flesh, and drink of your blood
so we are bound together as one.

Teach us to lose ourselves and find you
so through us it is you who lives and labors
joyfully we will die, we will laugh,
for now we live in you forever,
King of Kings and Lord of Lords.

BUT NOW IN CHRIST JESUS
you who once were far off have been brought near in the blood of Christ. For he is our peace, who has made us both one, and has broken down the dividing wall of hostility.

— *EPHESIANS 2:13-14*

35

Light In The Darkness

REALITY IS MEANT to sanctify us
the poor call us to Christ
wealth, power, praise, and position
lift us up into a world of thin air
we are called to reality
where Christ is crucified
to bury ourselves in the darkest, deepest wounds
of humanity
where there is sin and suffering, sickness and death
where there is hopelessness and despair, bitterness
and tears
into the deepest and darkest hell on earth
we are missioned to find Christ himself
where there is midnight meeting the dawn,
the light, Christ, merciless in his mission
of happiness, hope, love, and everlasting life

AND AFTER YOU HAVE suffered a little while, the God of all grace, who has called you to his eternal glory in Christ, will himself restore, establish, and strengthen you.

— 1 PETER 5:10

36

Carry His Cross

THE HEAVIER THE Cross of Christ
the greater is his love for you
you are his friend, he calls you
to build his rejected Kingdom
of the hungry, the naked, the wounded
the sick, the outcast, the prisoners,
the forgotten ones
you are his friend, he loves you, you love him,
you will do anything for him
he trusts you to carry the Cross,
the beatitudes that bring joy and happiness
as you descend among the forgotten ones
down the ladder, down, down
amongst those who live in hell on earth,
persecuted, abused, rejected, wounded,
you know there is Christ,
you know there's life,
among the suffering and dying you live,
and you will be lifted up one morn
by the angels to God's heavenly home

GREATER LOVE HAS no man than this, that a man lay down his life for his friends.

—*JOHN 15:13*

37

Follow God's Agenda

PERHAPS THE LORD is more present in the
poor than in
ourselves because we have cluttered our souls
we've cluttered our places, cluttered our lives
with too
many concerns for security and too big an agenda

we have such a long agenda that we block the grace
of God and the movement of the Holy Spirit in
our lives
we do not allow the doors of our souls to be open
to the Lord, we do not allow our souls to sing

the lives of the poor are not so cluttered, they live
each day by Divine Providence, they live according
to what is given to them, not according to what
they demand of life: blessed are the poor, he says

FOR GOD IS at work in you, both to will and to work for his good pleasure.

— *PHILIPPIANS 2:13*

38

You Are His Light

THE BEATITUDES ARE the lantern of our souls
within us the light shines bold and bright

"Come to me, come to me, the light of lights."

feeding the hungry, by Christ being fed
a drink of water, while quenched by his blood
clothing the poor, by his flesh we're enfolded
welcoming the stranger, by his loving hands,
visiting the prisoners, with his forgiving heart,
healing the broken-hearted, with his soothing
hands

NO ONE AFTER lighting a lamp puts it in a cellar or under a bushel, but on a stand, that those who enter may see the light.

— *LUKE 11:33*

39

Live God's Plan

WHAT IS GOD'S BLUEPRINT for his Kingdom here on earth?

that we make a world of his beatitudes
it is God's messengers preaching his Good News to the poor
welcoming the stranger, feeding the poor, clothing the poor,
giving water to the thirsty, loving our enemies and our persecutors,
forgiving sinners, distributing justice, distributing knowledge,
distributing goods and lands and the fruits of the earth,
offering kindness without cost or personal reward,
sacrificing our lives for others,
building community with Christ on the Cross,
loving and serving the poor and sinners unto death:
it is these that make us rich

TRULY, I SAY TO YOU, as you did it to one of the least of these my brethren, you did it to me.

— *MATTHEW 25:40*

40

Be A Faithful Servant

WE ARE HERE to bring light, to bring people to
see the purpose
of their lives, that men and women should not be
consumers
of dust and return to the dust and that be the end
of it all

we live, we die and we are judged
either—the Lord condemns us—you are not
worthy of my
Kingdom because you have not lived my truth

or—the Lord receives us happily, joyfully into his
Kingdom
—come, come and enter into my heavenly home,
for I was
hungry and you fed me, I was thirsty and you gave
me drink

MAY YOU BE STRENGTHENED with all power, according to his glorious might, for all endurance and patience with joy, giving thanks to the Father, who has qualified us to share in the inheritance of the saints in light.

— *COLOSSIANS 1:11-12*

THE MISSIONARIES OF THE POOR (MOP) take vows of poverty, chastity, obedience and free service to the poorest of the poor.

Father Ho Lung and the MOP priests and brothers surrender all rights to their own material possessions, bodily desires, will and remuneration for services rendered to the poor. They have no private possessions and no bank accounts. The MOP live in community, sharing all things in common.

The material needs of the MOP are supplied by the generosity of readers like you—readers who share their faith, embrace their mission and offer their own resources to serve the poor.

To learn how you can assist the MOP in their mission and join them in serving the poor, visit their website at www.missionariesofthepoor.org.

Or contact them at:

MISSIONARIES OF THE POOR USA
P.O. Box 29893
Atlanta, GA 30359
(404) 248-1197
www.missionariesofthepoor.org
mopusa@bellsouth.net

Spread the Faith with . . .

TAN · BOOKS

A Division of Saint Benedict Press, LLC

TAN books are powerful tools for evangelization. They lift the mind to God and change lives. Millions of readers have found in TAN books and booklets an effective way to teach and defend the Faith, soften hearts, and grow in prayer and holiness of life.

Throughout history the faithful have distributed Catholic literature and sacramentals to save souls. St. Francis de Sales passed out his own pamphlets to win back those who had abandoned the Faith. Countless others have distributed the Miraculous Medal to prompt conversions and inspire deeper devotion to God. Our customers use TAN books in that same spirit.

If you have been helped by this or another TAN title, share it with others. Become a TAN Missionary and share our life changing books and booklets with your family, friends and community. We'll help by providing special discounts for books and booklets purchased in quantity for purposes of evangelization. Write or call us for additional details.